An IIMS Self Help Guide

What A Marine Surveyor Needs To Know About

Small Craft and Superyacht Valuations

by
Capt Philip

1st Edition

Published by the International Institute of Marine Surveying

First published November 2016 by the
INTERNATIONAL INSTITUTE OF MARINE SURVEYING
Murrills House, 48 East Street, Portchester, Hampshire, PO16 9XS, UK

www.iims.org.uk

Copyright 2016 © International Institute of Marine Surveying

ISBN 978-1-911058-10-6

IIMS PUBLICATION
Item number: IIMS-10-6

All rights reserved. No part of this publication may be reproduced, stored in a retrieval system or transmitted in any form or by any means electronic, mechanical, photographic, recorded or otherwise, without the prior written permission of the publisher, International Institute of Marine Surveying.

Although the author(s) and publisher have made every effort to ensure that the information in this book was correct at the time of going to press, the author and the publisher do not assume and hereby disclaim any liability to any party for any loss, damage, or disruption caused by errors or omissions, whether such errors, or omissions result from negligence, accident, or any other cause. The author's views are not necessarily those of the publisher.

Printed by Mixam UK
mixam.co.uk

Front cover photo by Mike Schwarz

ABOUT IIMS

The International Institute of Marine Surveying (IIMS) is an independent, non-political organisation promoting the professionalism, recognition and training of marine surveyors worldwide.

The IIMS defines marine surveying as: "The service provided to maritime and transport organisations in general and the production of guidance reports for all other bodies connected with maritime operations or maritime trade".

The IIMS is the professional body for marine surveyors and has a worldwide membership of around 1,000 individuals in over 90 countries. It is the largest organisation of its kind and seeks to represent its industry to government and non governmental organisations such as the International Marine Organisation (IMO), Coastguards, insurance companies and ship owners.

The IIMS provides a range of services to its members, allied organisations and to the wider shipping and boating world, including:

- Maintaining a comprehensive database of qualified marine surveyors
- Professional training courses for marine surveyors
- A distance learning education programme in marine surveying
- The Report, a quarterly publication highlighting key marine surveying topics and news
- Conferences and meetings internationally providing a place for the marine surveying industry to meet
- Acting as an MCA approved vessel coding authority duly authorised by the Maritime & Coastguard Agency

www.iims.org.uk

CONTENTS

Chapter 1. INTRODUCTION 7

Chapter 2. DEFINITIONS 9

Chapter 3. THE VALUER 11

Chapter 4. SHIP vs SMALL CRAFT VALUATIONS 13

Chapter 5. THE VALUATION METHODOLOGY 17

Chapter 6. THE VALUATION PROCESS 31

Chapter 7. LIABILITY 33

Chapter 8. CASE STUDIES 35

ABOUT THE AUTHOR 39

Chapter 1.
INTRODUCTION

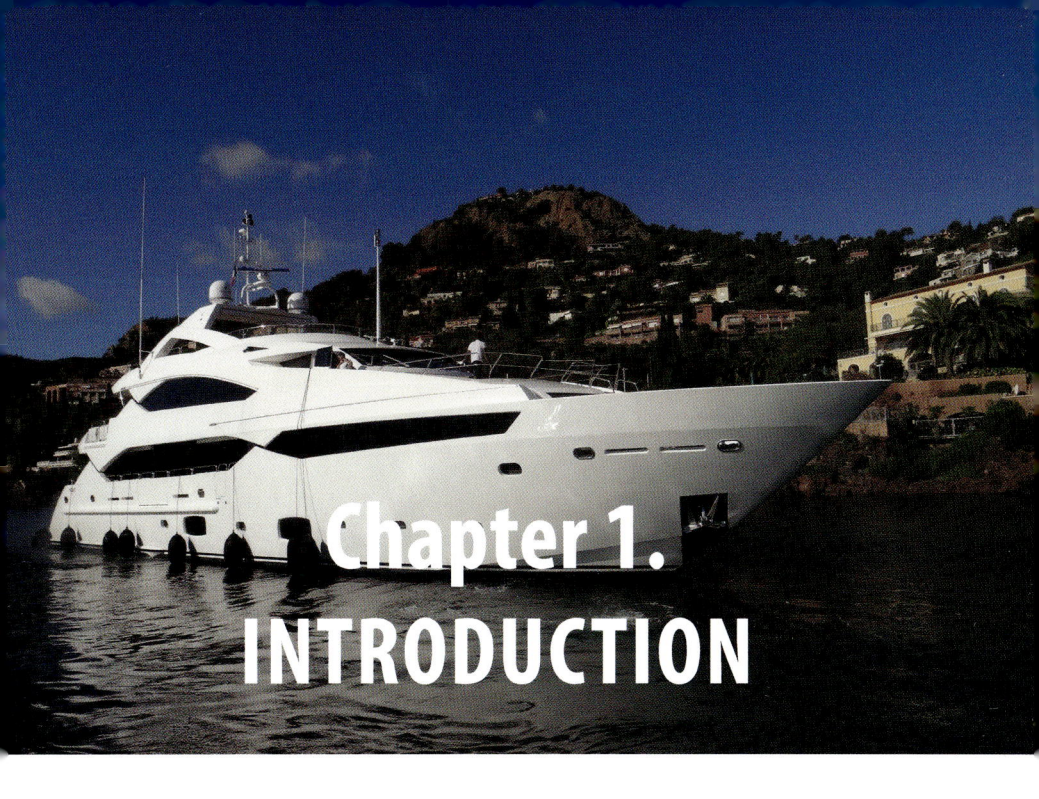

When deciding to write this guide I was reminded of a conversation with an in house marine surveyor for one of the leading marine lenders; during our conversation he mentioned that he found that although many small craft surveyors had the technical expertise to assess the general condition of a vessel, they often lacked, or misunderstood the discipline required of a professional valuer.

I hope that the approach I have outlined in this guide, in some way aids in addressing this perception. Just as with all aspects of the marine surveyor's craft, it is important to have a standard to measure one's conclusions against, and vessel valuation is no different, not least in order to protect one's liability.

The standard described in this guide is the IVSC (International Valuations Standard Council), Market Value Basis of Valuation SV1/2. I have attempted to breakdown the methodology used for valuations into manageable sections, and to approach them from a small craft surveyor's point of view; however, it should be said that it is the responsibility of the individual surveyor to ensure that he understands the requirements of his instructing client, and he carries out his professional work with due skill, care and diligence with the proper regard for technical standards expected of him.

I would like to thank the IVSC for permission to reproduce sections from the IVSC Standard SV1/2. Any surveyor who is serious about carrying out professional valuations should have current copies of the relevant standards. The IVSC can be contacted via the web on **https://www.ivsc.org/**

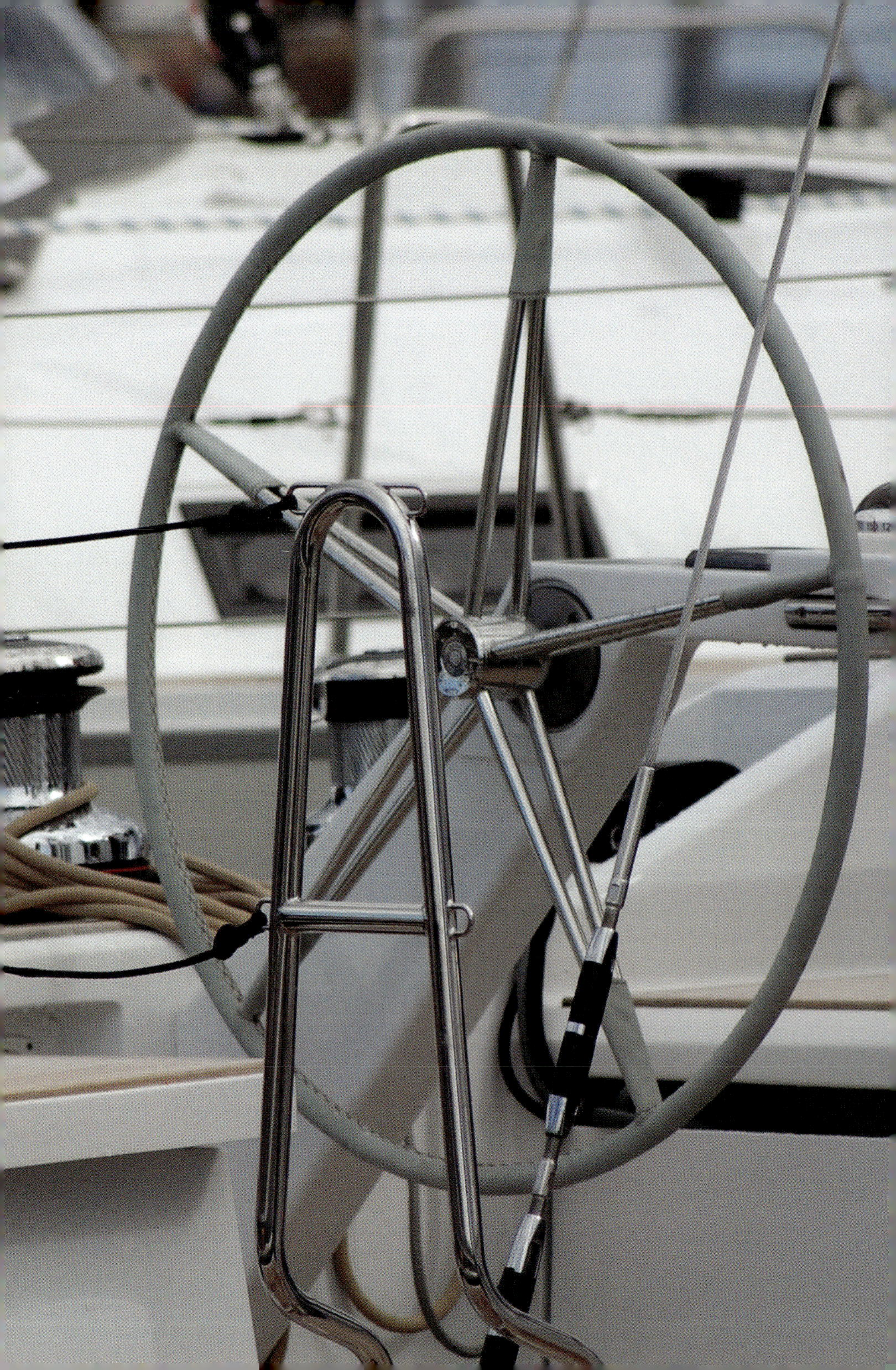

Chapter 2.
DEFINITIONS

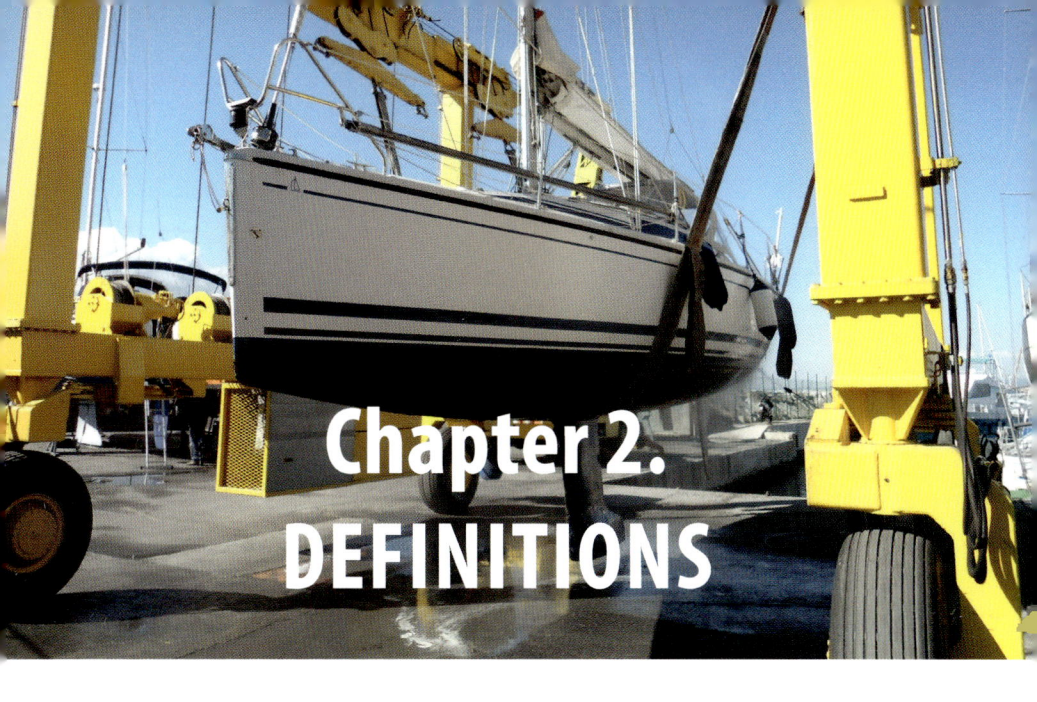

The following definitions are used throughout the guide; many will be already familiar to most Marine Surveyors.

IVSC: The International Valuation Standards Council (IVSC) is an independent, not-for-profit organisation that produces and implements universally accepted standards for the valuation of assets across the world in the public interest.

Basis of Value: The valuation method that is being applied - normally Market Value is used for marine craft. However, there are rare circumstances where Non Market Valuation methodology is applied.

Market Value: The estimated amount for which an asset or liability should exchange on the valuation date, between a willing buyer and a willing seller, in an arm's-length transaction, after proper marketing, and where each party had each acted knowledgeably, prudently and without compulsion.

Note: I have used the term *Market Value* throughout this guide rather than the term *Fair Market Value*, as although the terms are used interchangeably, the term *Market Value* refers to the price an asset would fetch, were it to be sold within a specific open market. This price is not necessarily equivalent to what the asset was purchased for, only what it is worth at the time of the valuation. The term, *Fair Market Value*, is often confused with the term Fair Value; this fair price may be lower or higher than the market price, depending on how much it is worth to the party buying it.

Market comparable method: Comparative analysis of the current S&P (sales and purchase market), of the same type or similar type of vessel.

Assumption: A statement on the condition of a vessel without a physical inspection being carried out, usually as a part of a comparative analysis; i.e. assuming the vessel to be in good working order and in the sound seagoing condition in hull and machinery which is to be expected of a vessel of its age, size and type, undamaged, fully equipped, and free of liens or encumbrances.

Small Craft Surveyor: A professional person who carries out inspections on vessels less than 150 feet LOA (or metric equivalent), which is private, pleasure, inland, river, coastal or commercial. (Definition provided by the IIMS).

Depreciation: Depreciation is the systematic reduction in the recorded cost of a fixed asset over a given period.

C&V, Condition and Valuation Survey: A C&V is primarily intended to assist insurance underwriters in making risk decisions. The survey has two primary purposes: (1) to identify the vessel, its equipment, condition and general value, and (2) to identify defects, damages or hazardous conditions that pose a potential threat to the safety of the vessel and its passengers; or any other such condition that is likely to result in loss or damage.

Valuation appraisal: A limited form of a C&V intended to provide a market valuation only, using agreed assumptions as to the seaworthiness of the vessel.

Replacement cost: In the insurance industry, replacement cost or replacement cost value, is the actual cost to replace an item or asset at its pre-loss condition. This may not be the market value of the item.

Actual cash value: Is the amount equal to the replacement cost, minus depreciation of a damaged or stolen property at the time of the loss. It is the actual value for which the asset could be sold, which is always less than what it would cost to replace it.

Seaworthiness: For maritime insurance purposes - a ship is deemed to be seaworthy when she is reasonably fit in all respects, to encounter the ordinary perils of the seas of the adventure insured.

Tort: A tort is a legal wrong, for which the law provides a remedy. It is a civil action taken by one citizen against another and tried in court.

Contract: A contract is an agreement giving rise to obligations which are enforced or recognized by law.

Diminution of value: Is a legal term used when calculating damages in a legal dispute and describes a measure of value lost, due to a circumstance or set of circumstances that caused the loss. Specifically, it measures the value of something before and after the causative act or omission, creating the lost value in order to calculate compensatory damages.

Chapter 3.
THE VALUER

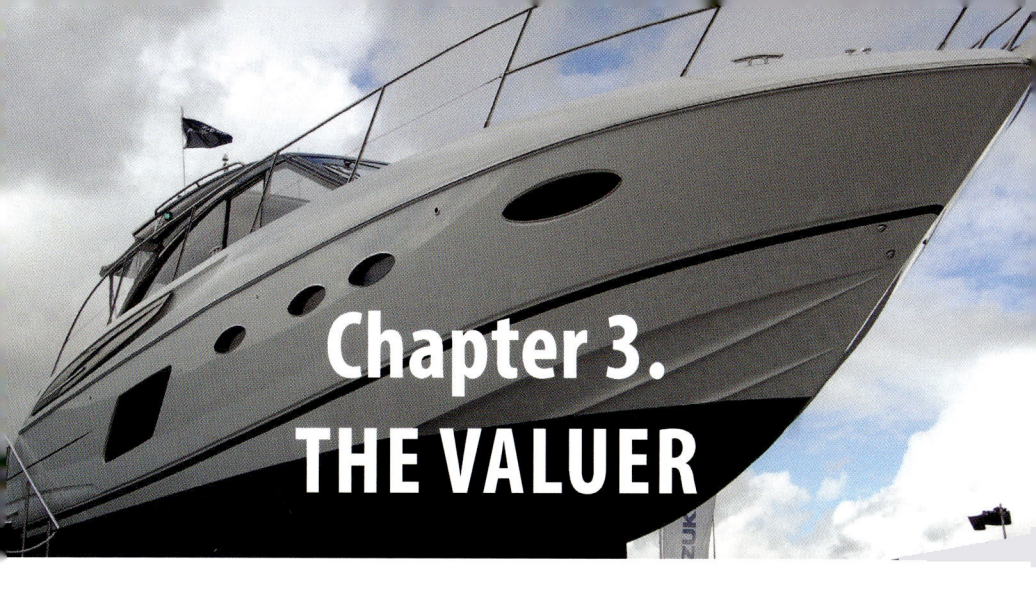

The role of the professional valuer is usually thought of with regard to property valuations; both private and commercial with the Royal Institute of Chartered Surveyors (RICS) being the UK body that accredits professionals within the land, property and construction sectors worldwide. In the USA, the American Society of Appraisers (ASA) is a multi-disciplined, non-profit, international organization of professional valuers who carry out financial appraisals on property, machinery, business and private assets. There are also valuation organizations in other parts of the world dedicated to maintaining high professional standards; again, mostly focused on property values. Business valuations are traditionally within the sphere of the accountant with the profession having its own organizations and societies dedicated to training and education.

Numerous books and literature have been produced over the years on the subject of valuations. The RICS Red Book is a yearly publication which contains mandatory rules, best practice guidance, and related commentary for all members of RICS undertaking asset valuations. One of the most well regarded publications is 'Valuation Principles into Practice' by Bill Rees, now in its sixth edition. Ship valuation has become a recognized profession with many ship valuation firms advertising their services on the internet, and there is even a 'Certificate of Vessel Valuation' via correspondence course now available. The aircraft sales and purchase market also has valuation companies providing up to date market values on all types of aircraft.

The role of the valuer within the pleasure boat market for insurance and loan purposes has traditionally been left in the hands of the marine surveyor with the assumption that with his skill and knowledge to assess the condition of a particular vessel, he should therefore be able to provide a market valuation. The sales broker on the other hand is expected to calculate a vessel's value for the sales and purchase market without having the experience to assess the vessel's full condition and seaworthiness. Whilst this balance can often produce an accurate market value, it can also in my opinion, often leave the interested parties uncertain as to the reliability and accuracy of the final valuation.

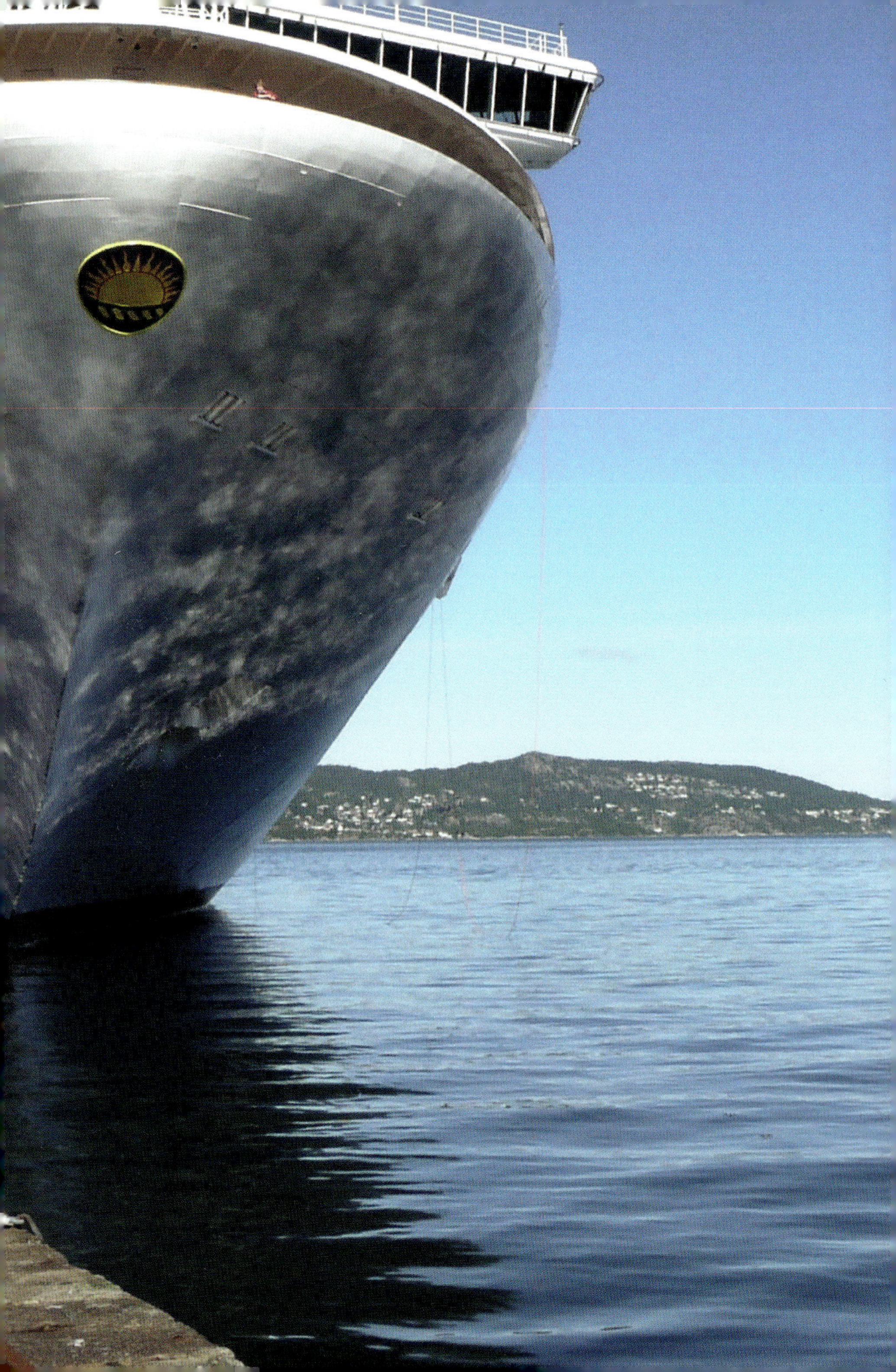

Chapter 4.
SHIP vs SMALL CRAFT VALUATIONS

Commercial Ships

It is worth spending some time looking at the commercial ship market as a background to small craft valuations. The ship broking market is centred on one basic principle, that a commercial ship, whatever its type, be it a ferry or a VLCC, has a finite life and therefore has an intrinsic value based on quantifiable figures.

For example, if a small crude carrier is 10 years old with an estimated life of 20 to 25 years, the remaining life span can be measured against its estimated potential future earnings and its scrap value at the end of its life. Once depreciation is applied; a market value can then be calculated after a comparative analysis of similar vessels in the relevant S&P market.

Indeed, some ship owners see trading in vessels as more profitable than actually operating them. This is a fairly simplified explanation as in reality various complicated algorithms are used by ship valuation appraisal companies to monitor the market place on a daily basis. It is worth mentioning that most ship valuations are 'desk' valuations, in that the valuer does not leave his desk when making the valuation and does not see the vessel concerned or any comparable sale vessel.

How then do valuers know what they are assessing? It is in fact a paper exercise; they work on a paper description of the vessel, type, age, class, builder etc. which is usually provided by the commissioning party along with market information contained in their own database, and with a set of agreed assumptions acceptable by both parties. Although there are some very reputable and independent ship valuation companies, it is also true that some ship brokers also issue certificates of valuation, with the obvious question arising of a conflict of interest. It has therefore become more common for lenders to request a condition report on the vessel to accompany the valuation, especially in today's volatile financial market.

Small Craft valuations

How do small craft valuations differ from the big ship market? The first and most important difference is that a small pleasure vessel has no intrinsic value, in that it has no calculable finite life, as in the *classic yachts* market for example. It could be argued that some small commercial craft such as river ferries and wind farm support vessels etc could be valued using the same methodology that is applied to large ships; however, the vast majority of small pleasure craft require a somewhat different approach.

The methodology used is a market comparable approach combined closely with a condition report from an independent marine surveyor. In most cases the valuation and condition report are provided by the same independent surveyor, with some of the larger surveying companies producing valuations relying on a surveyor's field report forwarded to an in house valuer. It is often the case that a client will request a valuation at the last minute during a pre-purchase survey. The surveyor then tags a half page comment including a valuation figure at the end of the report, sometimes with no extra fee involved. There is nothing fundamentally wrong with this, as long as the surveyor is aware that he may, at some point, be asked to justify his valuation; in the worst case scenario to a court of law in the event of a dispute involving a lender or insurer.

Reasons for valuations

There are several reasons why small craft valuations are requested and include:

- *Security for a mortgage or loan* - Banks require an independent appraisal of value.
- *Security for an existing loan* - Lenders need to be kept aware of the underlying value of their security.
- *Forced sale* - Courts require an indication of value as a reserve in the event of an auction.
- *Insurance purposes* - Annual accounts/audit, companies need to know their asset values.
- *Legal disputes between owning parties.*

When looking at the above it is obvious that the expectations of value, by the commissioning parties can vary greatly. For instance the insured value would not be expected to be the same value achievable from a forced sale. It is important that the valuer is aware of the instructing client's perspective and expectations, and he should remain objective and be clear which criteria he is using and why.

The purpose of the valuation should always be clearly stated in the terms of instructions in the valuation report, ensuring that the surveyor will have gone some way to protect his liability in the event at some future date, that the valuation is used for some other purpose by a third party.

The small craft sales and purchases market

Any discussion on the yacht and small craft market should begin with the role of the broker. There has traditionally been an uneasy relationship between the broker and surveyor with both sides intimating cases of corruption or incompetence. Whilst there are undoubtedly incidences of this type from time to time, as there are in any walk of life, the vast majority of brokers and surveyors are honest professionals.

We have all often heard the old chestnut; *"there are no qualifications required to be a marine surveyor, anyone can call himself a surveyor and set himself up in business!"* Since when is experience not a qualification? Experience is the surveyor's most valuable asset. In one sense the above statement is true, but it more easily applies to the lack of formal qualifications to be a yacht broker rather than the yacht surveyor. The broker is the one providing the glowing descriptions for all types and sizes of vessels, handling the sale contracts, dealing with client's deposits, whilst all the time operating under pressure to make the sale and get the commission!

One of the main aspects of the yacht brokers' work is to advise clients on the expected market value of marine craft; but it should not be forgotten that the broker is essentially a salesperson and he will in most cases advise clients that the advertised price is negotiable, sometimes very negotiable! Having said that, on receiving instructions, like most surveyors, I will look up the vessel or type of vessel on the internet and see what the *quoted* market price is.

The reason that a marine surveyor is asked to give a valuation and not a broker is twofold; firstly, the surveyor should be an impartial, independent professional with no conflict of interest. Secondly, if the property market has one axiom it is *location, location, location*; the small craft market maxim should be *condition, condition, condition*! It is the marine surveyor who, by applying his skill, knowledge and experience, can accurately report on a vessel's seaworthiness and general condition, which relates directly to its market value. However, as stated earlier, the marine surveyor may be an expert in his field but often does not have the knowledge or discipline required of a professional valuer, or the in depth knowledge of the sales and purchase market that a professional broker requires.

The small craft sales and purchase market is in effect tiered, firstly by size; over and under 24 meter LOA, then by type power or sail, high speed or a cruiser, and then by age. The same size rules tend to apply to brokerage firms with the larger firms dealing with the super yacht market, and the smaller brokers focusing on a particular LOA limit, with many specialising in sail or power.

The particular aspect of the small craft market that strongly affects the valuation process is its volatility; it is in essence a luxury goods market and therefore is quickly impacted by any recessionary trends, often with yachts being discounted at the first hint of a down turn. So it is very important that any surveyor carrying out valuations keeps abreast of market conditions. In fact, it is advantageous for a professional valuer to have a network of broker contacts he can approach for opinions on the marine market place. It is worth noting that the actual sale price of a vessel may in some cases be vastly different from the market value, in some cases by plus or minus 25% to 40%. This simply reflects the vagaries of a luxury goods market, where buyers and sellers make subjective personal choices. Indeed the fact that a particular vessel sells at a greatly reduced or inflated price may be known only to those involved in the actual transaction, and due to the confidentiality required from many buyers, the final sales price may never be known.

Chapter 5. THE VALUATION METHODOLOGY

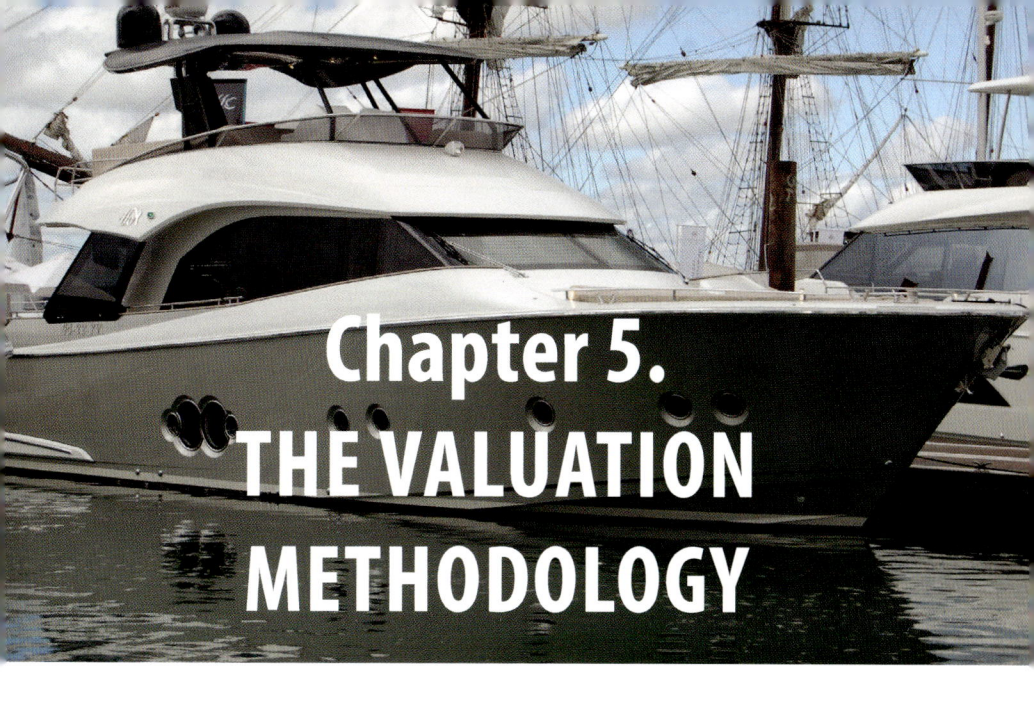

I consider the following to be the minimum content of a surveyor's valuation report. I do realise that the vast majority of small craft surveyors are only concerned with C&V (Condition and Valuation) surveys for insurance purposes which I will look at in more detail later; however, I do feel that having an understanding of the full valuation methodology will provide some underpinning knowledge that will add to better accuracy and more precise reporting.

Minimum Report Content:

- Scope and limitations of inspection
- Basis of value
- Vessel identity details
- General description of the yacht
- General commentary on the builders
- Commentary on the condition of the vessel
- Observations on the market
- Comparative analysis
- Valuation
- Depreciation
- Annual running costs
- Signature statement
- Photographic record

We can now look at this methodology in more detail.

Scope and Limitations of Inspection:

This is the standard statement of purpose that should be attached to any survey report. It is basically saying what the intentions were in carrying out the survey in the first place, along with the limitations of access encountered.

Here the surveyor can also add which parties were attending the survey, for instance, an assistant to the surveyor, the vessel's Captain and crew, or an owner and representatives were present. It may be relevant to mention the weather conditions, especially if the survey inspection is restricted by bad weather.

Of vital importance, to protect the author's liability, is a statement identifying the intended user of the report, normally restricted to the instructing client and not for use by a third party. Of course this does not prevent the surveyor's report eventually ending up in the hands of a third party; nevertheless, the surveyor will have gone some way to protect his liability in the event of a dispute.

Example:

THIS IS TO CERTIFY, I did attend onboard the Motor Yacht XXXX. The vessel was inspected at port XXXX, afloat, stern to, a limited out of water hull inspection was also carried out (one hour), whilst the vessel was held in slings. The intention of the survey was to ascertain the general condition of the vessel for valuation purposes. The survey was carried out in accordance with the agreed terms and conditions of the contract signed by the instructing client.

This report carries no warranty regarding ownership or any warranty regarding outstanding mortgages, charges, liens or other debts there may be on the vessel.

This report is submitted for the exclusive use of the instructing client and no liability will be accepted to any third party who may subsequently use a copy of this report, or any of its contents. Copyright remains with the instructing client and the undersigned Surveyor. This report should only be used for its intended purpose and the instructing client only has the right to disperse this survey with discretion.

The above should not be confused with the surveyor's standard terms and conditions (STCs), as these should have been signed by the client on acceptance of the instruction and should also contain the statement of exclusive use.

Basis of Value

There are several basis of value open to a professional valuer and it is vitally important to state which basis has been applied when making the valuation, although as a small craft surveyor the market comparable method (Market Value) would be the main approach. The following are some basis of value that may be relevant to the marine surveyor.

Market Value

Market Value is the estimated amount for which an asset should exchange on the date of valuation between a willing buyer and a willing seller in an arm's-length transaction after proper marketing wherein the parties had each acted knowledgeably, prudently, and without compulsion. This is the basis applied in most small craft valuations and will be looked at in more detail later.

Investment Value or Worth

The value of an asset to a particular investor or class of investors, for identified investment objectives.

Not really common in small craft valuations; however, there may be a case for this basis to be used from say a charter yacht with a syndicate of owners requiring an estimation of ROI (return on investment).

Insurable Value

The value of an asset provided by definitions contained in an insurance policy contract.

The actual insured amount is decided by the insurers. In the event of a claim the surveyor may be asked to provide a market value taking into account the cost to replace or repair, either a total or partial loss, less depreciation for age and condition.

Assessed Rateable or Taxable Value

Based on definitions contained within applicable laws relating to the assessment.

Although Market Value is often cited in this case, care must be taken to define the application, as the methods used may give different results from the MV method.

Depreciated Replacement Costs

Considered an acceptable method used in financial reporting to arrive at a surrogate for the Market Value for which market value is unavailable.

A method of valuation which provides the current cost of replacing an asset with its modern equivalent, less deductions for all physical deterioration, and obsolescence.

Salvage Value

The value of an asset as if disposed of for the materials it contains. – 'Scrap value'.

Liquidation or forced sale

The amount that may reasonably be received from the sale of an asset within a time frame too short to meet the marketing time frame required by the Market Value definition.

This basis is by definition going to be of a lesser value than what could be expected from the full application of the Market Value. It is generally not easy for a valuer to predict, because of the nature and extent of subjective and conjectural assumptions that must be made in formulating such an opinion.

There are other bases of value used in the appraisal process, especially with regard to company and business values and for accounting purposes; however, for the small craft surveyor, the basis of value generally used is the *Market Value* basis.

The IVSC standard

The following are the most important sections of the IVSC *Market Value* standard, used by the small craft surveyor and are worth looking at in detail.

The Market Value Standard

Market Value is the estimated amount for which an asset should exchange on the date of valuation between a willing buyer and a willing seller in an arm's-length transaction after proper marketing wherein the parties had each acted knowledgeably, prudently, and without compulsion. It is also understood to be ex taxes or any other cost of sale or purchase, although VAT can be added if requested.

The Estimated Amount

A price expressed in terms of money payable for the asset in an arm's-length transaction. Because the small craft market is very international, the currency used should be established at the outset.

On The Date of Valuation

Refers to the figure quoted by the surveyor, is time specific, and in fact could be argued that the moment he writes down the figure it becomes obsolete!

An Asset Should Exchange

Refers to the fact that a value of an asset is an estimated amount, rather than an actual sale price.

Between A Willing Buyer and A Willing Seller

Although both parties are motivated to sell or buy, neither party feels any outside influence on the proposed transaction. Both are willing to accept a price acceptable in the current market.

In An Arm's-Length Transaction

Defines parties that do not have a special relationship; for example, parent or subsidiary companies. The market value transaction is presumed to be between two unrelated parties each acting independently.

After Proper Marketing

Outlining that the asset should be on the market and exposed in the best possible manner, in order to effect its disposal.

Wherein the parties have each acted knowledgeably and prudently and without compulsion

This presumes that both the buyer and seller are reasonably informed about the nature and characteristics of the asset, and are motivated to undertake the transaction. In the case of marine craft, it could of course be the responsibility of the brokers involved to ascertain that the parties involved are reasonably informed.

Vessel Identity Details

A certificate of valuation should show at a minimum, the name, official number, and HIN (hull identity number), where registered, and type, commercial or pleasure, along with length, beam, and tonnage. It may also be relevant to give the present owners' details, although this may be confidential. A copy of the vessel's registration document can also be attached to the certificate of valuation as an annex.

If the valuation is part of a condition survey, the vessel identity details will form part of the full report; however, if the valuation is a stand alone appraisal, it would be prudent to include a summary of the vessel's main specifications.

The following large yacht sample layout will be familiar to most surveyors but it is worth remembering that an important part of the valuer's job is to accurately identify the asset he is applying the valuation to.

Vessel identity details

Name of vessel:	Gross tonnage:
Flag:	Nett tonnage:
Official number:	Propulsion systems:
HIN:	Generators:
Builder:	Fuel Capacity:
Year:	Fresh water:
Type:	Black water:
Material:	Oil Capacity:
Length:	Grey water:
Breadth:	Power AC/DC:
Depth:	Class:

General description of the vessel

When giving details of the vessel it is important to take into account that the client or the client's representative may have little or no knowledge of marine craft. This is particularly relevant when dealing with financial institutions, where asset value is of the prime concern, and it matters not whether the asset is a yacht, aircraft, fine art, or property. The extent of the description should reflect the size and complexity of the vessel:

Example A: From a 2009 new build valuation

The vessel is a semi production motor yacht built by Benetti Yachts in Viareggio, Italy, with exterior design by Righini and interior design by Zurreti. The hull and superstructure are built in fibre reinforced plastic. Permanent accommodation is provided for 10 guests in two double cabins, two twin cabins, and a double owner's suite. Crew accommodation is provided for; six crew, in two twin cabins, and two single cabins. Access to the aft deck is via a portside passerelle, external stairs from the aft deck lead to the upper and sun decks whilst side decks lead to the forward sunbathing area and foredeck. Sliding glass doors lead to the main salon and guest accommodation. - Continuing with a general description of the vessels interior layout etc.

Example B: From a 2016 C&V report

The vessel is a GRP production, aft cockpit, sailing yacht built by Bavaria yachts. Fitted with a deck stepped, mast head rig and includes a furling main sail and genoa. Accommodation is provided for 6 persons in one double, and one twin cabin along with a convertible salon berth for two. An adequately equipped galley is installed along with two bathrooms with showers and manual toilets.

How much detail provided is entirely for the individual surveyor to decide, taking into account the instructing client's requirements and the complexity of the vessel in question.

General Commentary on the Builders

The reputation of a builder can be very relevant to the value of an asset; for instance, Rolls Royce and Vauxhall both manufacture cars both have four wheels, an engine and interior seating; however, the expected quality and workmanship from one manufacture is vastly higher than would be expected from the other, and therefore, the perceived value should be higher based on reputation alone. The reputation of a particular make or model can also have an impact on a vessel's market value; of course this could be both positive and negative!

Example A: Extract from 2013 Valuation

Pershing S.p.a. has been designing, producing and marketing luxury 'open' motor yachts since 1981. The Pershing super yacht range is notable for its advanced construction methods, powerful engines and the use of surface propellers, hydro-jets and gas turbines. In 1998 the company joined the Ferretti Group; a leading enterprise in the luxury yacht sector, a move that has increased Pershing's presence in the American marketplace. The Ferretti group appears to have successfully weathered the global downturn and the Pershing brand of yachts has maintained its reputation of producing good quality vessels with modern innovative designs. The company has a strong international following for its products with several notable repeat customers.

Example B: Extract from a 2016 C&V

Sealine Yachts was a British boat builder founded in 1972 manufacturing small to medium range power boats. In the 1980's the company branched out into the larger end of the luxury market with some success; however, with the advent of the recent economic downturn, the company entered into administration in 2013.

Example C: Extract from a 2015 Valuation

Nautor Swan is a Finnish sailing yacht builder founded in 1966, over 2,000 Swan yachts have been produced, ranging from 36 to 131 feet in length. They have consistently maintained the highest reputation in the industry for building quality luxury sailing yachts. The firm employs about 400 staff, and a similar number of indirect staff. The company is dedicated to plug and mould fabrication and the lamination of all Swans' hulls using an advanced, and fully computerized milling machine to shape the moulds. In 2002, a new yard, close to the sea was opened. The new yard is dedicated to the assembly of 'Maxi' Swan Yachts, from the 'Swan 60' to the 'Swan 100'. Since 1998 a group of investors has controlled and managed Nautor's Swan, and continue to push forward innovations, and changes intended to maintain Swan yachts at the forefront of the international sailing world.

Commentary on the condition of the vessel

This part of the process is where the small craft surveyor should feel most comfortable, and where he gets to ply his trade; the only decision to be made, is to what extent the inspection should take. I have found that most surveyors have a very clear cut idea what a full pre-purchase survey should entail; but seem to be somewhat vague when it comes to a condition and valuation inspection.

I am reminded of a comment made by that venerable marine surveyor Mr Jeffery N. Casciani-Wood in reply to an underwriter's complaint that his C&V reports were too involved. *"Tough, I'm the surveyor and they are my reports, therefore my liability"* The point being, the surveyor is expected to give his professional opinion as to the general condition, and therefore the safety of a marine craft, along with providing a market valuation of the vessel, whilst expected to accept any liability involved in giving that opinion!

When the marine surveyor states in his report that he finds the *"vessel seaworthy and fit for purpose"* or more usually: *"if the recommendations noted in the above report are completed, the vessel will be in the opinion of the undersigned surveyor, seaworthy and fit for purpose."* What exactly is he saying? How much exposure to litigation does this statement have? It is worth exploring the term seaworthiness and the implications involved when making the statement. Although the term *"seaworthy"* does not have any legal foundation, it is widely used in the marine insurance world.

The Maritime Insurance Act 1906 defines Seaworthiness as:

(1) In a voyage policy there is an implied warranty that at the commencement of the voyage the ship shall be seaworthy for the purpose of the particular adventure insured.
(2) Where the policy attaches while the ship is in port, there is also an implied warranty that she shall, at the commencement of the risk, be reasonably fit to encounter the ordinary perils of the port.
(3) Where the policy relates to a voyage, which is performed in different stages, during which the ship requires different kinds of or further preparation or equipment, there is an implied warranty that at the commencement of each stage the ship is seaworthy in respect of such preparation or equipment for the purposes of that stage.
(4) A ship is deemed to be seaworthy when she is reasonably fit in all respects to encounter the ordinary perils of the seas of the adventure insured.
(5) In a time policy there is no implied warranty that the ship shall be seaworthy at any stage of the adventure, but where, with the privity of the assured, the ship is sent in an unseaworthy state, the insurer is not liable for any loss attributable to unseaworthiness.

Section 4 - Is of the most relevance to the small craft surveyor: *A ship is deemed to be seaworthy when she is reasonably fit in all respects to encounter the ordinary perils of the seas of the adventure insured.* It is the *'Surveyor's'* report that the insurers are using to aid in assessing this risk. This being the case, the scope that the inspection takes should be to his satisfaction as a professional marine surveyor, not to satisfy an underwriter who perhaps is too busy to read past the first few pages.

A comment from an underwriters claims deck:

The hull survey for insurance purposes should target those areas most of interest to the yacht underwriter. The most specific items of interest in this survey are (1) recommendations affecting the safety and seaworthiness of the vessel, (2) the new replacement cost <u>and estimated current sound value of the vessel</u> and (3) the surveyor's opinion as to the vessel's suitability for her intended service. Unfortunately the surveying profession often takes a circuitous and verbose route to provide these rather simple facts. In the best of all possible worlds, the hull survey for insurance itself should adequately describe the vessel in no more than two pages of text with a separate listing of the significant recommendations. The recommendations should be crisp, concise and address a specific condition…

Unfortunately not many of us live in the best possible world and need to protect our liability! One way to reach a compromise on this is to write the report with the summary and conclusion on the first page followed by the recommendations on the second and the body of the report following on with a certificate of valuation as an annex. This means that the underwriter need only refer to the first couple of pages if he so wishes; however, the body of the report still contains the surveyor's conclusions in some detail in order to protect his liability at a later date if required.

What then is the main difference between a C&V and a Pre-Purchase survey?

In my opinion a C&V is a PP survey without the sea trial or possibly the haul out. I am aware that a lot of small craft are surveyed for pre-purchase purposes without a sea trial, or even a bollard pull, but this in my opinion should be a rarity not the norm; few of us would buy a car without a test drive! There is the case where the vessel is of a certain age and a hull inspection is requested. If the yacht is already on the hard, the scope of the inspection can be very limited indeed, given that the surveyor may not be able to run up any machinery, and cobwebs in bilges are not the normal sea going state of affairs! Of course any restriction to the scope of the survey should be recorded in the report; however, this should be balanced against the need to carry out instructions as fully as possible.

This is a list of survey requirements from one of the leading yacht insurance companies:

Underwriters require that the survey report has been carried out within the last five years and must include (as a minimum), an evaluation of the following points where appropriate:

1	The condition of the hull beneath the waterline and topsides. Any sign of impact, distortion or any form of flexing, or delaminating. If moisture readings are taken is there any significant water ingress into the laminate. If the hull is steel or aluminium, hull thickness measurements will be required
2	The condition of the internal hull, bulkheads, stiffeners, keel attachment and support structure
3	The condition of the keel and external keel joint
4	The condition of the rudder, stern gear including the shaft and stern gland/ shaft seal, supports struts, the p-bracket, cutlass bearing and propellers

5	The condition of decks, superstructure and deck fittings
6	The condition of the mast and spars and age and condition of the standing and running rigging
8	Suitability and condition of ground tackle (number and weight of anchors, chain and warp and attachments)
9	Condition of the steering equipment. If wheel steering, is the mechanism (including quadrant, cables, hydraulics) in good condition. Is there an emergency tiller or other emergency steering arrangement available?
10	Can the vessel be secured against theft, i.e. do the main access hatches have locks
11	The gas (LPG) installation conforms to current safety standards
14	The condition of the electrical installation including the condition and stowage of the batteries. If there is an (AC) shore power installation, is it protected by a residual current device?
15	The condition of the engine installation and fuel supply
16	The condition of the sea valves and through-hull fittings
17	Are the number and type of bilge pumps adequate for the vessel
19	Is the fire fighting equipment onboard adequate for the type of vessel? Are the extinguishers in service date?
20	Are there adequate emergency flares on board?

The above list would give a good idea of the sea worthiness of the vessel; however, this needs to be balanced against other factors that affect the value, such as the cosmetic condition and appearance, along with any upgrades to standard equipment and inventory.

To summarise then, the reason that a marine surveyor and not a broker or accountant is asked to carry out a Condition and Valuation survey, or a Valuation appraisal, is that surveyors are expected to have sufficient technical knowledge to make a considered opinion as to the general condition of a marine craft, and balance this opinion against a knowledge of the marine market in order to reach a financial valuation that the instructing client can rely on. This being the case, the marine surveyor should make his own decision as to the scope of the survey required to reach his opinion, and to mitigate any risk of future liability.

Observations on the Market

I would not expect the average small craft surveyor completing a 10m sail boat C&V survey report to go in to a detailed analysis of the yacht sales and purchase market; however, it is worth bearing in mind that as professional surveyors we are expected to be able to measure and justify our recommendations, therefore making a statement of value is no different than making a statement on a piece of faulty equipment. The question *'how you arrived at the valuation?'* still needs to be answered, therefore, adding a short comment on the prevailing market conditions may be of assistance in explaining conclusions.

The small craft sales and purchase market over the last ten years has been extremely turbulent to say the least, with many well known boat builders going out of business and others being purchased by foreign investors and hedge funds. This coupled with volatile oil prices, and terrorism concerns, makes the process of valuing perceived luxury assets extremely difficult. However, there is no doubt that the market value of any asset is directly related to the financial health of the market concerned, and this in turn is affected by more worldwide economic factors.

Here are three extracts from commentaries used in valuation reports to highlight the relevant market conditions.

Example A: 2011 Extract from a commentary on the world wide large super yacht market

Since the world wide recession began in 2008, the market in luxury yachts has become extremely depressed with large numbers of used vessels on the market, and with considerable numbers of yacht builders going out of business. There is often optimistic talk from yacht brokers and builders of the market gaining momentum; however, approximately 4000 yachts of over 30 meters are on the market, and worldwide sales are calculated to be between 20 to 30 yachts per month, with prices down in some cases by 40% from 2008.

The backlog in used boat sales is mainly due to lack of finance being released by the lenders and willingness of builders to take used vessels in part exchange for new constructions.

Example B: 2015 Extract from a commentary on the UK boat building industry

The performance of the UK boat building industry has been hampered by the economic downturn over the past five years. The deterioration of the industry since 2008-09 was caused by poor economic conditions in the United Kingdom and in key overseas markets. Domestic economic conditions have become more buoyant over the past couple of years, but issues remain in some key export markets, notably the European market and as a result, revenue remains volatile...

Example C: 2013 Extract from a commentary on the Mediterranean small boat market

Due to the worldwide financial crisis in the last few years, the used small boat market has been very depressed with a large stock pile of previously owned boats available at heavily discounted prices, especially in the Mediterranean region.

As may be perceived from the above extracts, the author is, by the emphasis on the prevailing S&P market conditions, attempting to justify a somewhat lower valuation than his client may be expecting!

Market Comparative Analysis

When comparing one vessel against another in order to reach a conclusion regarding its value, there are several important factors to take into account:

Type: Not just motor boat to motor boat and sail to sail, but commercial or pleasure is also important.

Model: Fly bridge or open, engine upgrades etc.

Age: A new list price is a good starting point, and boats of the same year of build are ideal, but 1 or 2 years either side can still be relevant.

Condition: The condition of the comparative vessels will be normally an unknown and an assumption on the vessel's condition will usually have to be used, which must be clearly stated in the report. The condition of the vessel being valued should normally be following a physical inspection.

Inventory: Upgrades of AV/IT equipment, new sails, engine etc.

Location: The S&P market say in Greece and in the UK will have differing pricing levels.

Recent sale prices: New and used.

Recent advertised prices: When making comparative analysis, it is important to state whether tax is included in the price and that the examples used are from a similar region. There are various resources available that the professional valuer will use to aid in making a vessel comparative analysis including:

- Personal knowledge
- Sales broker contacts
- Internet sales advertising
- Dedicated vessel pricing web sites such as; Soldboats.com, BUCvalu, Nada, *etc.*

It is also prudent to include a waiver such as:

Whilst every effort has been made to accurately reflect current market pricing, no guarantee can be made regarding the accuracy of the quoted sales figures and any advertised prices can be expected to be subject to discounting.

Example A: Extract from a valuation appraisal of a 40 meter Superyacht

Similar vessels recently sold 2015 (ex Tax):

Benetti 44m -year 2011, lying Italy	sold 03/2015 €14million
CRN 43m -year 2010, lying France	sold 06/2015 €12million
Sunseeker 39m -year 2009, lying France	sold 08/2015 €8.7million
Sunseeker 37m -year 2008, lying France	sold 05/2015 €9.9million

Example B: Extract from a C &V of a Sealine 31

Sealine 310 -1995- lying UK. Sold 2015	€59000 inc. Tax
Sealine 310 -1995- lying UK. Sold 2015	€50000 inc. Tax
Sealine 310 -1995- lying Greece. Sold 2015	€30000 inc. Tax

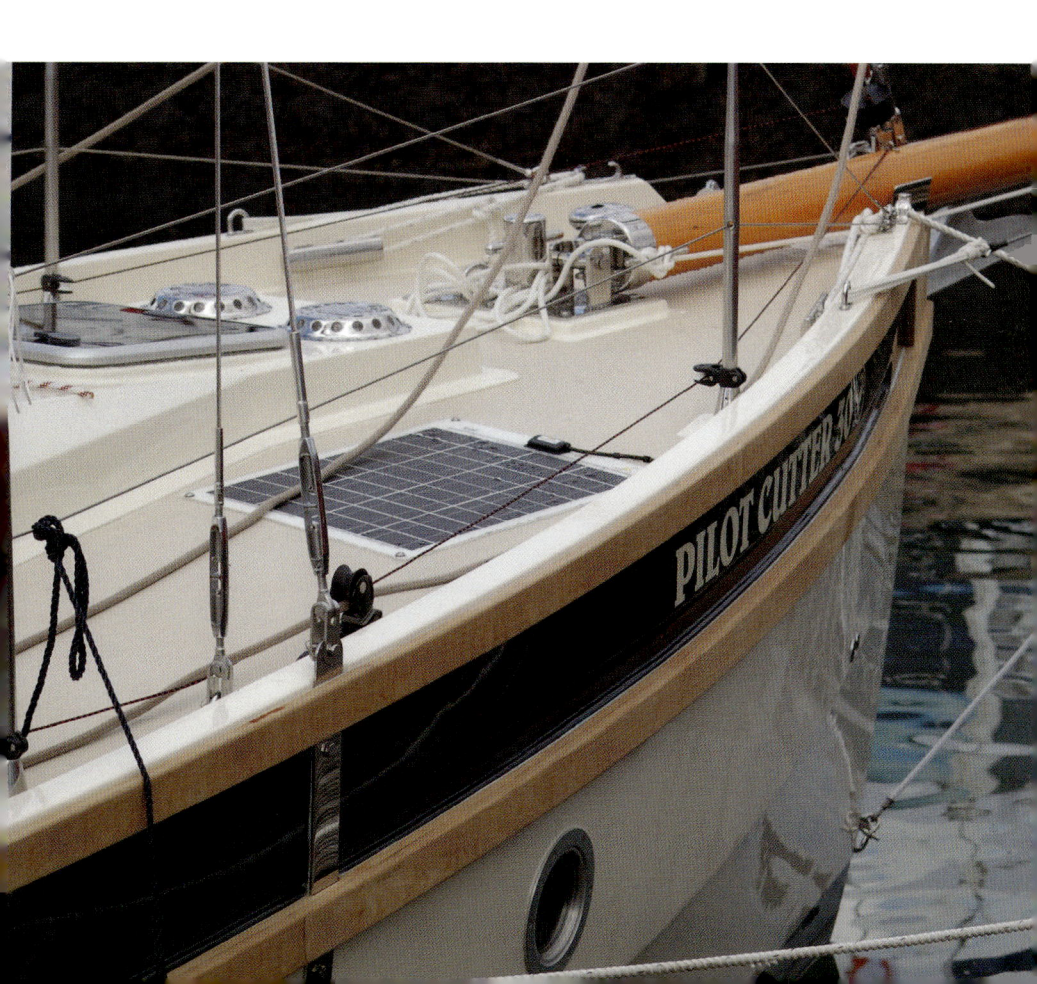

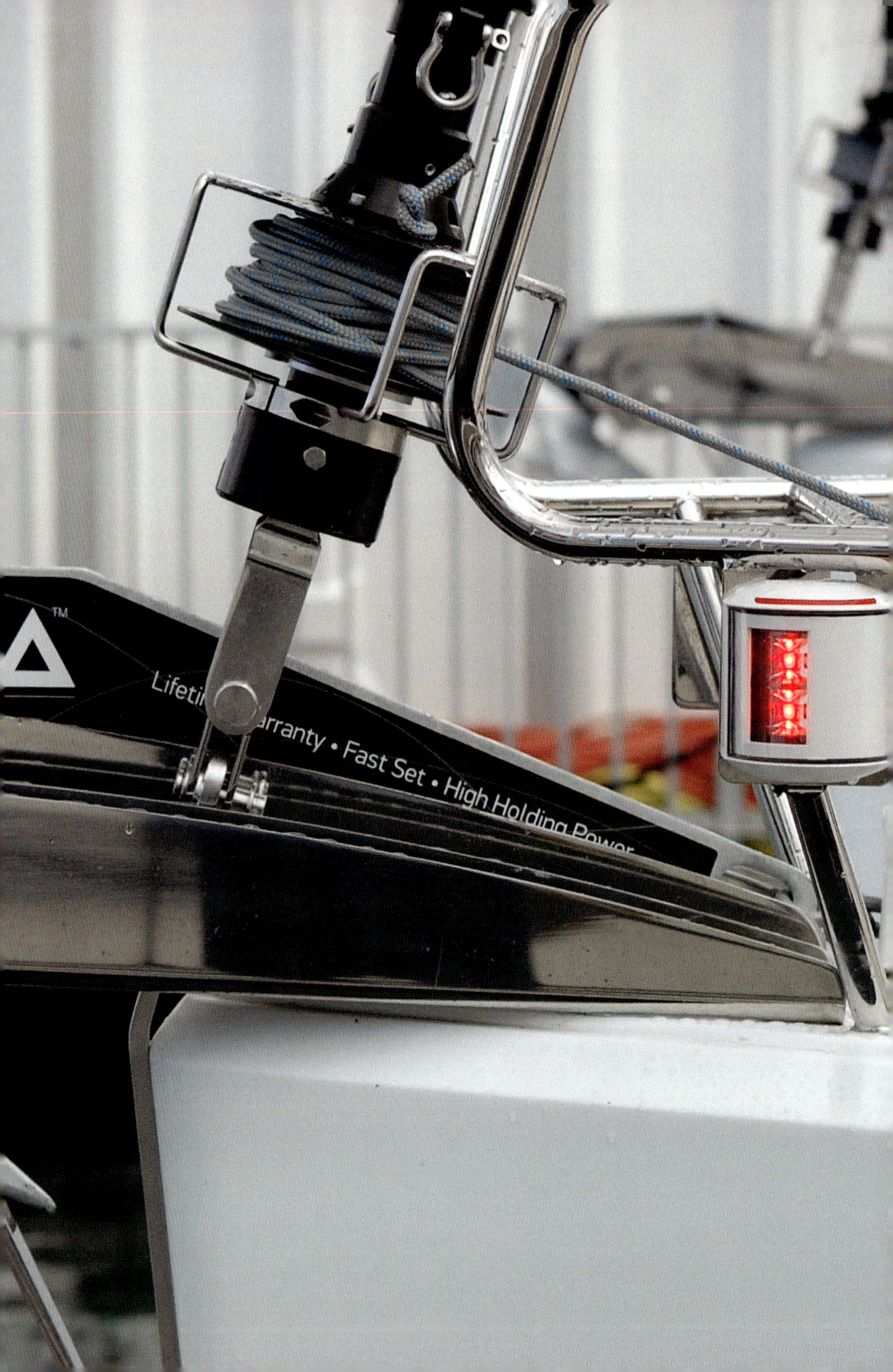
Lifeti arranty • Fast Set • High Holding Power

Chapter 6.
THE VALUATION PROCESS

Although I am sure the following process is familiar to most experienced surveyors, I feel it is worth reviewing:

1. If possible the surveyor should look up the vessel in question, normally via the internet, and decide if it is within his survey capabilities. For instance, it may be of a size or material outside of his experience.
2. If the vessel is outside of the surveyor's normal scope it would be prudent to contact his PI provider for advice.
3. Agree the terms of engagement with the client and forward a contract along with T&C's (terms and conditions) for signature.
4. Ask the client for copies of any relevant paper work on the vessel i.e. Registration document. Technical papers etc.
5. Carry out the condition survey inspection on the vessel.
6. Once back at the desk collate all the available information that will assist in reaching a considered opinion as to the vessel's value, this should include:
    - The surveyor's opinion on the condition of the vessel.
    - Comparative price analysis from available resources. Internet, media, and personal contacts.
    - What are the present relevant market conditions?
    - What is the market reputation and financial position of the builders?

Once the final estimate of the vessel's value is reached, the author should ask himself: *'is the valuation justifiable?'* Remember that it is easier to answer awkward questions from a disappointed owner, or an irate broker than reply to a cross examination from an opposing counsel!

Although the methodology behind the valuation process is to a great extent an application of known factors, there is by the very nature of the process an element of intuition involved; so the final question the surveyor should ask himself when looking at the arrived figure is: *'does it feel right?'* The author will balance this feeling against the condition of the vessel as he surveyed it and the prices found in the S&P market.

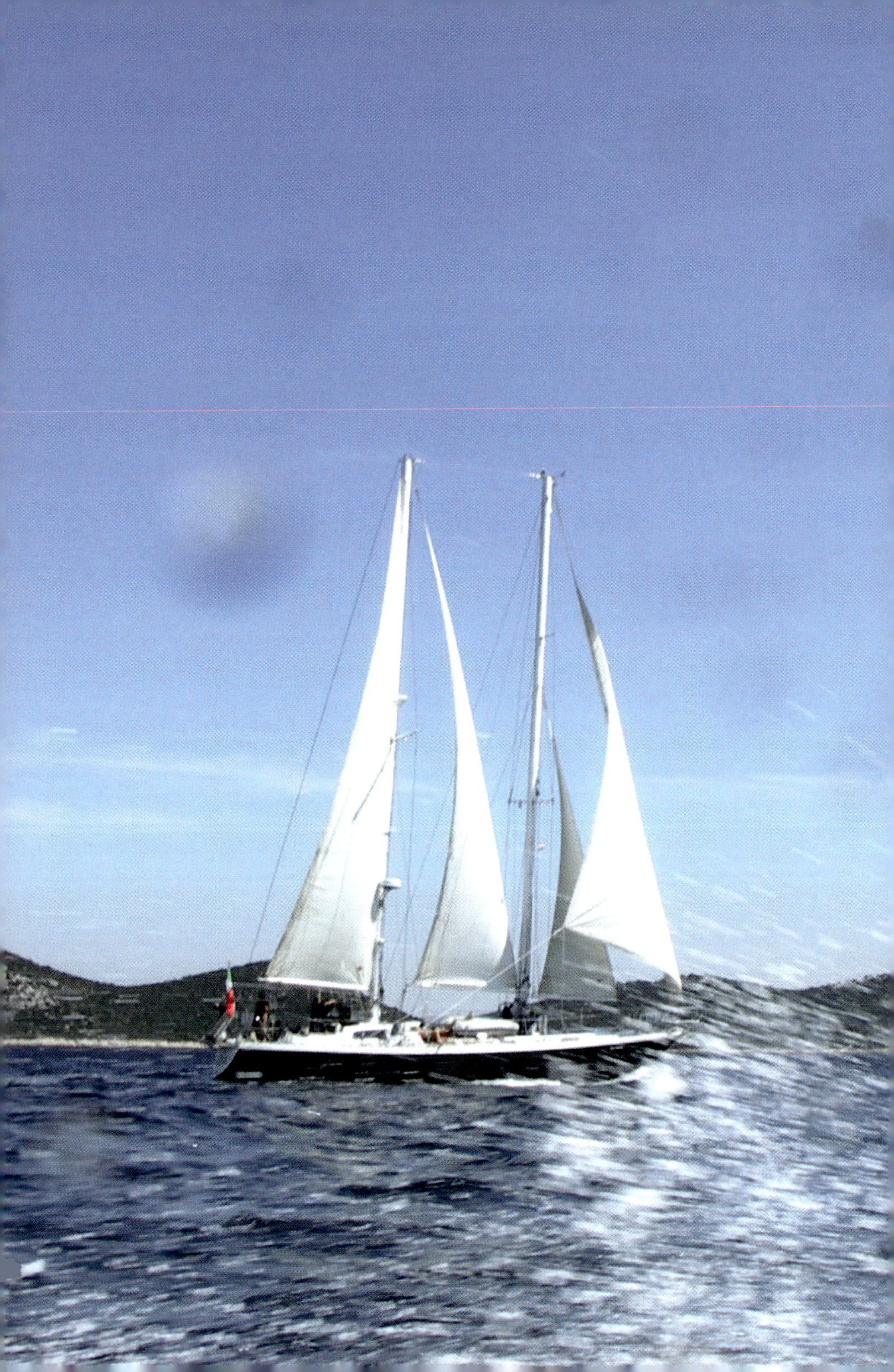

Chapter 7. LIABILITY

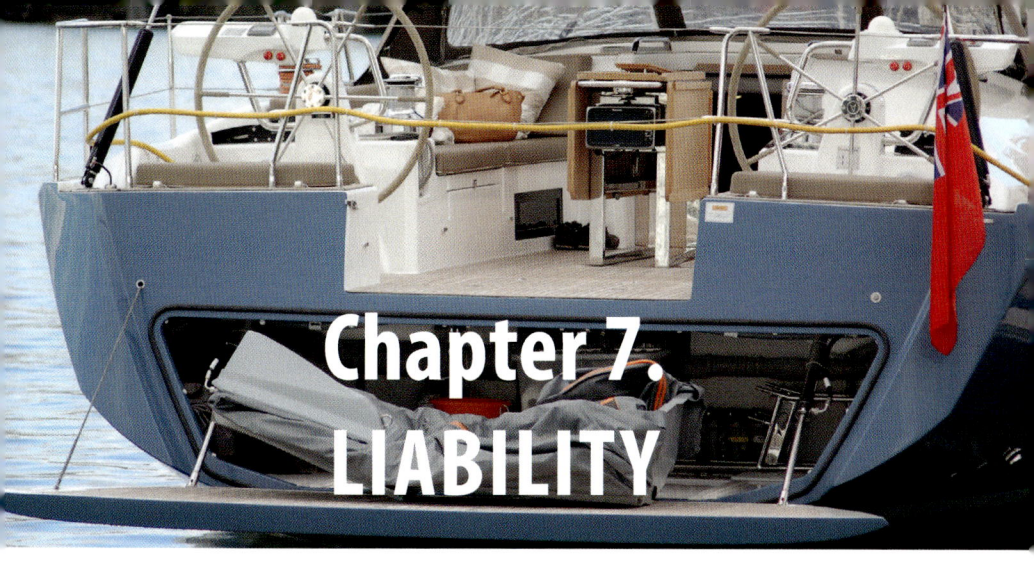

Generally speaking, marine surveyors are exposed to liability under both the law of contract and the law of negligence. The exposure of a marine surveyor to liability under the law of contract will vary depending upon the terms of the agreed contract between the surveyor and his client. However, courts will generally imply that the survey should be conducted by a surveyor with a degree of skill and competence which is generally exercised by marine surveyors with regard to the type of survey in question.

In other words, when accepting the instruction, the surveyor should fully understand what has been agreed to in the terms of engagement and be competent to carry out the work. Not really an unreasonable demand from a considered professional!

We should look at the exposure under the law of contract. To bring a claim for negligence, a claimant needs to prove three things:

1. That the Surveyor owed a duty of care to the claimant.
2. That the Surveyor breached that duty of care.
3. The claimant suffered a loss.

Normally in marine survey cases, the focus is on the loss, but the first thing that needs to be established is was there a duty of care owed? This then goes back to the original contract between the two parties in whatever form it took, whether verbal or written, both are viable.

The relationship between the client and surveyor can be proved by the agreed contract between the two parties and therefore a duty of care established. In the case of a condition and valuation survey however; there is a third party involved, namely the insurer or lender, therefore, is there a duty of care owed to the third party? The answer is yes! It has long been established that a third party can bring a claim if they relied on the advice of an expert.

The specific point here is that even if the marine surveyor has what he thinks is a water tight contract between himself and the client, it does not prevent a third party, such as an insurer, from making a claim against the surveyor if the third party feels that the surveyor has breached his responsibility for a duty of care.

The other consideration to take into account with regard to contractual agreements is that no matter how many disclaimers and limitations to liability a surveyor includes in his contracts, he may be still liable under the Unfair Contracts Act 1977, which does allow disclaimers, but only if they are reasonable. There are various tests used by courts in order to establish these such as:

- Would it be reasonably practicable for the third party who relied on the report to have obtained their own?
- Was there sufficient time?
- What was the cost?
- How difficult is the task being undertaken by the surveyor?
- Who instructed the surveyor?
- Who paid his fees?

It is worth remembering that the disclaimers and limits of liability a surveyor includes in his contracts and T&Cs, may only be a first line of defence, and a third party may decide to claim subrogation or invoke the unfair contracts act.

This is a very important consideration when carrying out C&Vs or Valuation surveys, so the surveyor should beware of his liability when a client asks at the last minute to tag on a valuation to a pre-purchase report at the request of client insurers.

The specific liability issue with regard to valuations is diminution of value. Diminution in value is a legal term used when calculating damages in a legal dispute, and describes a measure of value lost due to a circumstance or set of circumstances that caused the loss.

The circumstances of loss in a C&V case could be either a gross miscalculation by the surveyor of the market value. This would only be evident if the vessel was offered immediately for sale and all the relevant market conditions remained the same, and of course the new valuation would have to be proven to be correct. Or, if during the condition survey a major structural or machinery issue was missed, that would affect the seaworthiness, and therefore the value of the vessel.

From a recent court ruling: *The reasonable cost of repairing a damaged chattel is prima facie evidence of the diminution in value caused by the damage, whether or not it is in fact repaired.*

The exposure to liability of marine surveyors in general, depends on several factors. The location of the surveyor, as different countries has different liability laws. The type of work being carried out, and the business structure the surveyor operates under i.e. Limited Liability Company, or self employed sole trader for instance.

It cannot be overstated that the best protection a surveyor can have with regard to mitigating his exposure to litigation is a good quality and relevant Professional Indemnity policy, supported by access to legal advice if needed.

Chapter 8.
CASE STUDIES

Case ONE: 20 year old 12m GRP sailing vessel

The owner has been directed by his insurers that a condition and valuation survey is required in order to renew his cover. He goes on the internet and finds a local surveyor to carry out the inspection and arranges the haul out. He also tells the surveyor the boat is presently insured for £30,000, and that there is no history of a previous survey. The surveyor finds several defects that would effect the seaworthiness of the vessel including, jammed sea valves and out of date fire extinguishers. More importantly, during the haul out several areas of osmotic blistering around 5mm in diameter are discovered.

When the surveyor comes to write his report he makes a list of defects with accompanying recommendations, most of which can be put right at a minimum cost; however, the osmotic blistering is a different issue altogether because although the blistering does not affect the vessel's seaworthiness, it does affect its value. The surveyor quite rightly states that the blistering at this early stage is not a serious issue, and recommends several options; including that an osmosis treatment could be carried out on the hull at some future point.

The surveyor then proceeds to calculate what he thinks is the present market value of the boat taking in to account the defects list and the cost of an osmosis treatment. After a comparative analysis of the same or similar boats advertised for sale, or recently sold, he reaches a market value figure of £22,500. With a loss in value mainly reflected by the hull blistering, and the present state of the S&P market. The insurers agree an insured value with the boat owner on the proviso that the items listed as 'A' defects on the surveyors list, or those that affect its seaworthiness, are immediately addressed. The only concern that the insurers have about the osmotic blistering, is the reduction in insured value, as small osmotic blisters would not compromise the hull integrity and therefore not heighten any risk to seaworthiness.

The issue here is to ensure that any defects discovered during an inspection are divided into those that affect the market value of the vessel, and *'run of the mill'* easily repairable defects. In the above case, the owner carried out all the surveyor's recommendations, but decided to live with the osmosis, accepting the value of the boat would be greatly reduced if he came to sell.

I have often seen C&V reports stating *"if the recommendations noted above are completed I would give a Market Value of XXXX."* This may be okay with one or two small defect items; however, the Market Value provided by the surveyor should reflect the condition of the vessel at the time that the survey was carried out. It would be better to say *"if the recommendations noted as 'A' above are completed, I would deem the vessel XXXX to be seaworthy and fit for purposes as a XXXX, and I estimate the current market value to be XXXX."* The actual insured value of the vessel is a matter between the insured and the insurers.

Case TWO: 5 year old 14m GRP commercial charter motor yacht

The surveyor has been instructed to carry out a full pre-purchase survey along with a market valuation; including expected depreciation and running costs. The Survey is completed including a sea trial and a haul out; and no major defects are discovered by the surveyor. After completing the pre-purchase survey report, the surveyor begins drafting the certificate of valuation, his main points of consideration are:

- The difference in value of a commercially coded yacht with a charter history, against a private, pleasure vessel in the same condition.
- The value comparison between similar commercial vessels on the market.
- The effect of general wear and tear and extended machinery hours of a commercial charter yacht with regard to depreciation.
- The increase in running costs of a charter yacht.
- Potential earnings.

At first glance it is easy to fall into the trap of assuming a higher value would be placed on a commercial yacht rather than a private one, because of its earnings potential. However, this must be balanced against the depreciation caused by the increased use including, machinery maintenance/replacement, and cosmetic wear and tear. It is very easy to get bogged down with what is essentially an accounting process, not within the surveyor's remit as a valuer, and end up giving financial advice rather than an objective opinion. This goes back to being very clear with the initial instructions and terms of engagement.

The most direct approach would be:
- Make a financial comparison between similar advertised and recently sold commercial vessels, and between similar private ones. For clarity, show these figures in the report, but give only one final valuation based on the specific vessel valued.
- Calculate running costs at a <u>minimum</u> of 5% of the vessel's value.
- Calculate deprecation based on the vessel's age in which it should have depreciated in value from new of between 30% and 40% over 5 years, and to be projected to be a minimum of 5% per annum for the next five years, and then increasing exponentially.

In the above case, the buyer pulled out of the deal due to a dispute with the sales broker over inflated potential earnings. The surveyor was asked what he considered to be the potential yearly income from charter; however, the surveyor quite rightly declined to comment, stating it was outside of his area of expertise and not part of the initial terms of engagement.

The lesson here is to be very clear about what the surveyor is being asked to do and to stay within the agreed limitations. Although the opinion of the surveyor as a valuer is an integral part of the transaction between the buyer and seller, he should not be part of the negotiations! The surveyor has been engaged to give his professional expert opinion, and once that has been given he should no longer be involved.

Case THREE: 10 year old 40 meter privately registered Super Yacht valued at £10 million

The surveyor was asked to provide an urgent quotation for a market valuation of the vessel by a yacht management company.

Prior to preparing the quotation, the surveyor had to look very carefully at the terms of engagement, his main concern was the time constraints. He would have only one day to inspect the vessel whilst she was moored stern to in a marina, so in essence he was being asked to do a walk through inspection. He carefully drafted his responses to the prospective client, indicating he was willing to carry out the valuation; however, prior to accepting the instructions he had some questions:

- What is the valuation for, sale or forced sale, insurance or finance purposes?
- Has the vessel been maintained in class?
- When was the last haul out?
- Is she fully crewed and operational?
- Are copies of all technical papers and insurance documents available?
- Are maintenance records available for inspection?
- Has she been on the market and if so for how long?

Having received most of the answers to his queries, the surveyor contacted his PI provider for confirmation that he had sufficient cover for a vessel of this value; he was informed he would have to increase his cover on a one off basis with a premium of £200 and provide a copy of the terms and conditions associated with the instruction. Having tied up all the loose ends the surveyor accepted the instruction and completed the valuation to the satisfaction of the client. It should be emphasised that the valuation report contained the agreed assumptions regarding machinery condition and restricted access which related to the limited time frame.

The main points to consider in this case are to ensure that both parties fully understand and accept the limitations being imposed, and that any potential liability is mitigated by checking that the surveyor has sufficient PI coverage.

Case FOUR: New build 37 metre Super Yacht

The instructions received from the bank are to provide a valuation on a 37m super yacht nearing completion, prior to the final loan instalment drawdown. The construction of the vessel started two years previously in 2008; however, since then the marine industry had suffered a catastrophic downturn due to the world wide recession, with many builders going out of business and a glut of yachts on the sales market.

The surveyor/valuer considers the following points before accepting the instruction:

- The original purchase price was agreed by the buyer prior to the recession and may not reflect its present value.
- The original loan was agreed by the lender and secured against the vessel prior to the downturn.
- The amount borrowed will have been paid out to the builders in staged payments during the construction period with an expected 25% outstanding as a final payment.
- The quality of construction may have suffered due to the financial downturn.

The surveyor accepts the instruction and arranges an appointment with the builders to visit the yard and inspect the vessel. He first meets with the yard's project manager and discusses the progress of the build, and the outstanding works to complete along with the expected timeline. He is also given copies of class technical papers. He then visits the vessel, accompanied by the owner's build supervisor and goes through his snag list. On returning to his office, the surveyor prepares the valuation report including; a commentary on the builders and their apparent financial stability, the quality of the build as seen, a comment on the forecasted delivery timeline and he includes an observation on the present super yacht sales and purchase market. The final valuation figure is as expected, several millions less than the initial purchase price.

Here we have a case of *'don't shoot the messenger!'* It should have been obvious to all concerned, that the value would be considerably less than the purchase price due to the downturn. The fact that the valuation figure runs the vessel into negative equity in the millions of Euros is irrelevant to the valuer *if*, of course, he has his numbers correct.

The valuer's job is to ensure that he lays out all the facts in a clear, concise, and logical manner, that is easily understandable by all concerned, and that his conclusions clearly justify his final valuation.

The role of the valuer is a contentious one at the best of times, and attempting to value something like a yacht that is often considered by the owner to be his pride and joy, or a potential for bankruptcy, can be a difficult and a nerve wracking process for a surveyor. I hope that the advice given in this booklet aids in some way, small craft surveyors to provide more accurate and justifiable valuations.

ABOUT THE AUTHOR

Captain Phil Duffy

Phil Duffy lives in the South of France and is the managing director of Interface Marine, a yacht and boat survey company established in 2006. The company carries out all types of survey work on small boats to Super Yachts, along with vessel valuations. Phil initially trained as an engineer before following a career at sea spanning 30 years on both sides of the Atlantic, including Master and Chief engineer on Super Yachts up to 50 meters, dive operations in the Caribbean and Central America, and as Master on Commercial High Speed Ferries.

He has worked in shipyards as both a project manager, and build surveyor on large yacht projects in France and Italy. He also owned and operated a RYA training centre in France, and taught as an MCA approved lecturer in Navigation, Safety, and Engineering. He is quoted, however, as saying that his *"most valuable experience gained towards becoming a successful small craft surveyor, was with five years spent as a charter boat skipper in the Caribbean in the early nineties, when it wasn't unheard of to sail overnight to find a fax machine, and if something broke you had to quickly learn how to fix it!"*

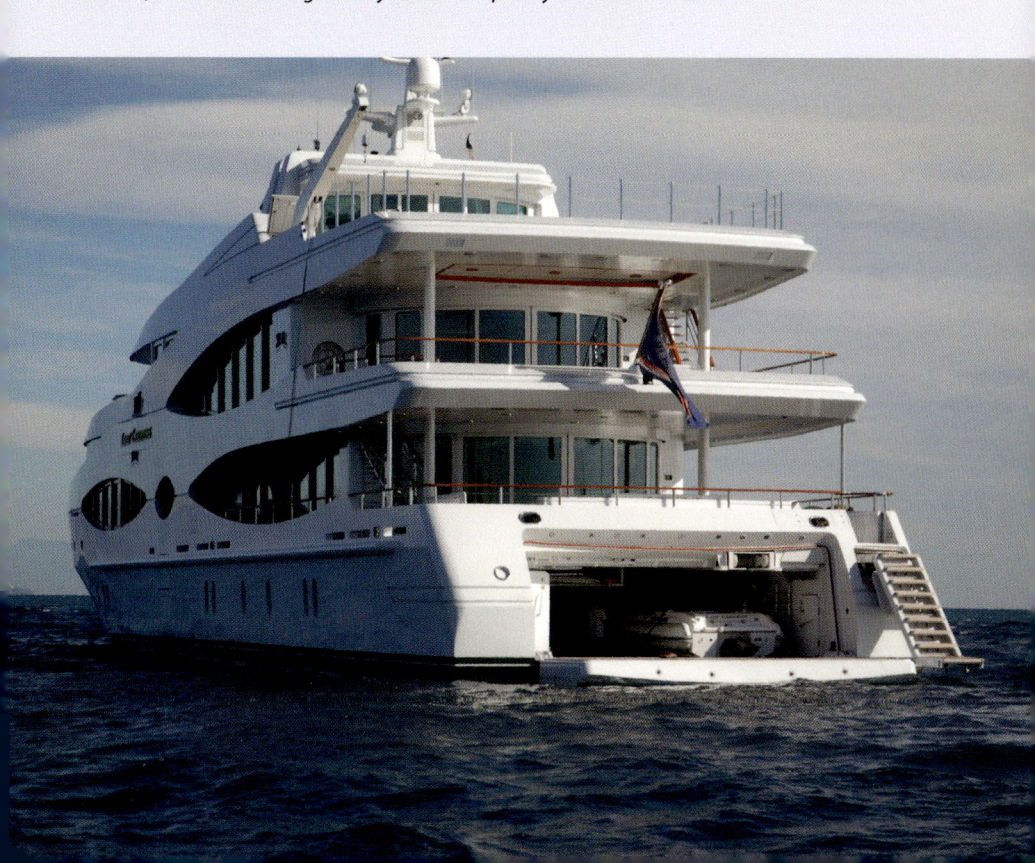

Follow IIMS on social media.

On Twitter:
@IIMSmarine

On LinkedIn:
Search for - International Institute of Marine Surveying discussion group

On YouTube:
Search for - MarineSurveying IIMS or go to www.youtube.com/c/MarineSurveyingIIMS

www.iims.org.uk

An excellent resource with everything you need to know about marine surveying in one place...

International Institute of Marine Surveying
Tel: +44 (0) 23 9238 5223
Email: info@iims.org.uk

Member Login   Student Login   Surveyor Search   View Videos

Welcome to the IIMS   News   About ▾   Membership ▾   Education ▾   Vessel Coding ▾   What's On ▾   Media ▾   Boat Owner Info ▾   Contact ▾

Welcome to the IIMS

ABOUT IIMS
The International Institute of Marine Surveying (IIMS) is an independent, non-political organisation promoting the professionalism, recognition and training of marine surveyors worldwide.
Read more »

Surveyor Search
Surveyor Name

Company Name

Country
Angola
Antigua
Argentina
Australia

Visit the IIMS web site soon!
www.iims.org.uk

Marine Surveying Academy

MARINE SURVEYING ACADEMY

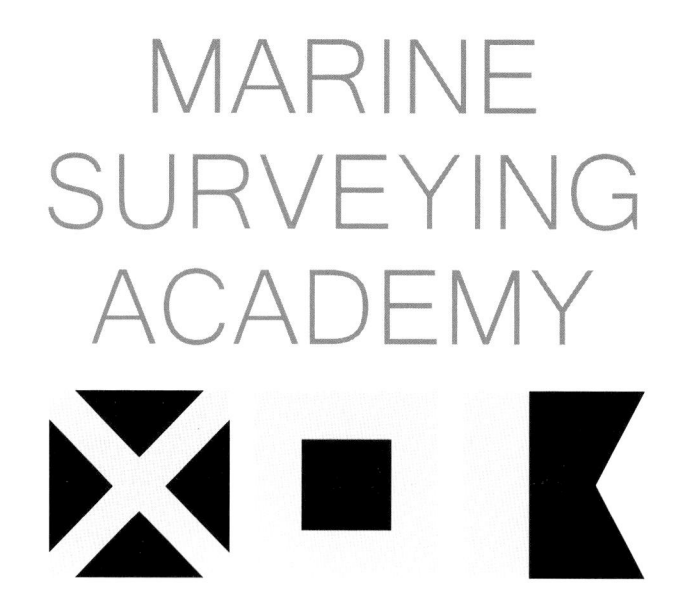

Dedicated to excellence in marine surveying education, training and accreditation

www.marinesurveyingacademy.com